T0034571

Thick with Trouble

ALSO BY AMBER McBRIDE

Gone Wolf

We Are All So Good at Smiling

Me (Moth)

Thick with Trouble

Amber McBride

Penguin Poets

PENGUIN BOOKS
An imprint of Penguin Random House LLC
penguinrandomhouse.com

Copyright © 2024 by Amber McBride
Penguin Random House supports copyright. Copyright fuels creativity,
encourages diverse voices, promotes free speech, and creates a vibrant culture.
Thank you for buying an authorized edition of this book and for complying with
copyright laws by not reproducing, scanning, or distributing any part of it in
any form without permission. You are supporting writers and allowing
Penguin Random House to continue to publish books for every reader.

Page 103 constitutes an extension of this copyright page.

LIBRARY OF CONGRESS CATALOGING-IN-PUBLICATION DATA
Names: McBride, Amber, author.
Title: Thick with trouble / Amber McBride.
Description: New York : Penguin Books, 2024. | Series: Penguin Poets |
Identifiers: LCCN 2023030229 (print) | LCCN 2023030230 (ebook) |
ISBN 9780143137474 (trade paperback) | ISBN 9780593511541 (ebook)
Subjects: LCGFT: Poetry.
Classification: LCC PS3613.C2764 T45 2024 (print) |
LCC PS3613.C2764 (ebook) | DDC 811/.6—dc23/eng/20230928
LC record available at https://lccn.loc.gov/2023030229
LC ebook record available at https://lccn.loc.gov/2023030230

Printed in the United States of America
1st Printing

Set in Sabon Lt Std
Display is Gotham and Bucanera

Designed by Catherine Leonardo

for the ancestors (always) . . .

They asked me if I was guilty
& I answered, not to myself.

—MARY G. HARRIS

I was riding a black horse bareback while smoking a pipe—
he saw me & fell.

—CHASSIE GARLAND

I don't want no worriation in my life.

—BERNARDINE McBRIDE

ROLL CALL: NEW TAROT NAMES FOR BLACK GIRLS

Call us something lovely
      mischief changing robes.

Call us hardened honey's brownness
      on the tip of the tasting spoon.

Brown hands cradling inherited softness
      or head cook, in a country church, hymning.

It's cold, darling. Come inside, make a cream-colored psalm of me.
      Call me gospel—I don't mind harboring millions of maybes at once.

Call us steak knife to clean meat from between teeth
      or steak knife to skin prey. Pray we don't snare you.

Cornbread crafted from spoiled milk or nickel-nicked knuckles.
      Fault lines haunting thighs. Crimson eggs nesting, in wait, between breasts.

Been called liars & midnight's evil twins. Deceits blossom like fungi—
      Black girl will hatch a long red snake-thing—a bloody cord
        that strangles on command.
      Black girl will <u>Sin</u> with anything with half a heartbeat—even a dis-ease.

That's fine, honey, call us Pestilence's hands
      slowly—edging Atlas—
          the reason he begs
             & drops it all.

Call us *end of days* or *pretty despite the Blackness.*
      Come into my soft coffin, my mouth buzzing flies.

Touch my heat-strum, one more time,
      I don't mind, I offer the death card to everyone.

Been called <u>trouble</u>
    that good
        good kind.

The (Troublesome) Poems

ROLL CALL: NEW TAROT NAMES FOR BLACK GIRLS

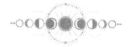

† Card One †

THE DEVIL'S SISTER (reversed)

† Card Two †

THE EMPRESS WITH A WHIP

† Card Three †

THE HERMIT WOMAN NAMED GRIOT

† Card Four †

THE DEVIL'S SISTER (upright)

† Card Five †

THE MAGICIAN-EST

Thick with Trouble

Card One

THE DEVIL'S SISTER (reversed)

the devil was made

from the rib of his sister

the mistress of <u>Sin</u>

THICK

Noun: In the <u>thicke</u>t of it we are just
the limbs & blossoms of chocolate vines stretched
       & strained & plucked & left.

           Adjective: <u>Thick</u> legs, nose, toes.
               <u>Thick</u>-built, strong as broken-twice bone.

                    Adverb: <u>Thickly</u>
                    swaying down
                      the boulevard.

Colloquial: Damn, they <u>thick</u>.

Poem: {Haint}

The night hag is haunting (again)
holding men down in bed with her <u>thick</u> hands.
Paralyzing them before asking,
    if you didn't like it, why didn't you scream?

Her lantern is unlit, cellar oil won't feed it—only blood.
She smiles, knife-bleeding his throat
life rivering down his neck.

Lantern finally lit, a <u>thick</u> line of red
slithers to the closet—stuffed with bloody garments,
                <u>thick</u> with secrets.

THE BIRTHING OF ME

inconveniently late to my own arrival / one day double-stitched & kissed into next full moon / might of stayed stuck forever / in my tiny universe (prideful already) inspecting my own clenched fist / I may of split my Mama in two / if not for the inducement / then me clawing out too fast / like some wrinkled wild creature in a horror film that you pity instead of hate / I clawed with tiny nails already daggered / slashing glass (born ready for <u>trouble</u>) / took first full breath frowning / if I had teeth I would of sucked them / thinking *this living thing ain't for me* / (still not sure) if this living thing is for me /

there was blood / but there is always blood / & shrieks sonic & soulful / but there is always song at a birth / panting & hollering as clear as wind chimes in a decaying mansion / you know they used to tell women not to scream / to let their pain multiply silently in their mouths without breaking the seam / fuck the seam / how can delivering a soul from a soul be anything but audaciously audible / maybe that's it / I didn't want my spirit to split from my Mama just yet / after that every step is laced with lonely / never connected with anything for more than a hasty collection of seconds again /

did you know in the south old wives' tales say late babies are second-soul born / very late babies' souls stretch a red string through the centuries / only anchored while forming / so I arrived (again) at the start with no knowledge of before / calmer than the science that makes fog do its foggy thing on weighty mornings /

& I arrived darker / by many shades than my Mama / darker than most thought I'd be / aunties saw pictures & said, *the blood must of sunk into her skin / she baked for too long /* they gossiped *she shoulda been born early / heart barely crafted like her sister's /*

I was too late to be fashionable / too pissed to cry / when I was motionless for a stack of moments there were more screams / my Hoodoo grammy says, *birth is a battle sometimes babies ain't ready to holler* / when the doctor slapped me / once then twice / I glared him down / with eyes too big for my tiny face / bloody from my first skirmish / looking back if had words / if language arrived as easily as breath / I might of said *I'll crawl into you next / I'll grow & gorge you / make you waddle & pee every 11 minutes / honey I'll split you in two . . .*

11 YEARS OLD (BLEEDING)

I.

i thought to stick my own hand
in myself, to tug the heartbeat out.

kinda like that boy, remember him—jack
who stuck his thumb in a pie & pulled out plum—
i'd birth a melting red apple, like that hen
that birthed golden eggs, except they won't
clap for me.

II.

an auntie told me,
between chews of chitlins,
it's your own damn fault you started so early,
you was born late, every extra day
in the womb counts as a year.
i clutched my stomach afraid.

it hurts, i whined.
it should, was the reply.

it was summer
& the sun was ripe
so i stumbled outside
sprawled like a lost starfish
on the sea-green grass, screamed
take it out into the wet air.

bled out.
right on the innocent dirt.
left a feast for the soil—
a red apple birthed from me.

SKULL HILL BAPTIST CHURCH

Is where I first saw a naked man
       (it's not like that).

I was in the pew & the pastor
       was sweatin' while I sucked
on the peppermint southern grandmas magick
from their Sunday church purses.

My stockings stuck to my thighs
       & my dress stuck to my stockings
& the mint stuck to the roof of my mouth.

The sun stamped shadows across my legs
       that felt cool, which is not how the sun works
& when I glanced up from my sweaty
stockings, from my stuck place in the pews
I saw a naked man.

A naked man with snakes hanging below his navel
& bones popping like wings from his back—
The letter *S* branded on his chest
       & his eyes frostbit my skin,
made the places he gazed
cold as Christmas snowstorm.

I swallowed my peppermint, started choking
& grandma (annoyed) hit my back three times
& when I looked up there was nothing.

The hazy man with snakes growing
between his thighs was gone
& the Black pastor's spittle sprayed as he said,

      & women have <u>Sinned</u> more than most.

Which means Black women because white
doesn't live within these walls.

Pastor watches me,
like he knows what I do
to myself at night.

ALBA & WHIMSY (1999)

I grew like a sap between two
oak trees named (Alba & Whimsy).
>Their roots massive crop circles in
>>my grandma's front yard.

When dusk dripped in
fireflies bejeweled Alba & Whimsy—
>mimicked the heavens
>SOS-ing constellations
>>that were too flickering to record.

Between (Alba & Whimsy) I ate pineapple
until my tongue swelled, until the night swelled
>with the sporadic sound of hundreds
>of chirping violinists.
Beneath me, their roots twined tighter
& with the right breeze, their leaves sometimes kissed.

Back then the ground told me secrets.
I knew things, like how it often stormed,
but only in the realm between (Alba & Whimsy).
>When their roots were angry with each other
>>they bickered underfoot. I knew they were afraid.

Some nights, rain boots in hand & honey offering in tow
>I would raise my sleep-soggy body
>>from bed & exit through the Dutch door
>>>to hush their underground thunder.

Between (Alba & Whimsy) I became a seashell
placed my hands over my ears & listened to the rain
>echo against my arms.

Until I could hear bees rumble inside me
      & my bones crackled & swelled with moss.

        Until, one day, they were hacked down to stumps.

GROWN-ISH BLACK GIRL LIVING ALONE WITH WHITMAN

These are the days that must happen to you.

—*WALT WHITMAN*

I.

Whitman wants me to seed roses in my bed. Be calm, he croons,
let the paint fall thoughtless off banisters, watch the moon quarter
                                    then halve & expand & contract.

Being twenty, I had time. We name each moon like a newborn child,
we spend months reading naked. He tells me my legs are stunning,
rests his head on my chest, I work at the tangles & pick out
                                    the twigs in his white pages.

Because we don't need clothes, I have almost emptied my closet twice.
No use: I love dresses too much. Whitman decides dresses are flowers,
so seeing as I never planted any I can keep them. So, we keep them,
                                    all of them, even the least flower-like.

He runs my bath
            & explains the generosity of water.
                    Rain has no stake
                            in anything,
                                    but still it falls.

He runs my bath
            & I slide down
                    until my mouth is covered.

Whitman says to understand you must be thirsty, so everything must go,
boxes of letters, sketches of full moons, spoons, even the champagne.
I leave the bath, drink the champagne, burn the sketches. The spoons
                            are outside on the windowsill collecting lectures from rain.

We paint my nails green; he massages my feet with cocoa butter.
With all this water I would have hoped to have grown fins by now,
to settle in a loch or a monster-less bay—to change into something other.
Whitman says that's not how water works.

It cleanses; it doesn't morph.

II.

Like most theories, I find the theory of abandonment messy.
Like a seam sliced & oozing sap. Whitman runs my bath (again)
& I think of Ophelia & stones & sliding under until the water holds my nose.

I think of living there, face half water-blur,
      my hair like a black mamba's body inking in every direction
          deadly mostly to itself.

III.

Whitman hauls me out of the water before I grow gills
(because that is not how water works)
      he says my hair, medusa-souled, made the water Sinful.

We don't need shoes, we are letting dirt in, soft, cool, untamed & complete.
I wonder how we will stay warm
      with only dresses & books. We will burn the sketches, he says.

The ones I swallowed & kept hidden (full-mooning) in my appendix.
      The ones I watered too thoroughly & digested too well.

The ones that cleave to me.
Whitman says, we might have to burn you too.

IV.

You see, I prefer the cold.

Whitman prefers rolling
toward a spine that springs
toward him each morning.

To be safe I refrain from baths.
        My moon-soaked appendix can't be trusted
with even the smallest tides.

V.

Whitman is angry—he tells me this is a usual mistake.
Which means a girl walks into a bar & finds the death card?
Which means that glue can't stop bleeding?

The thing is, I don't bleed anymore—
I started so young
        I bled dry years ago.

I am trying to tell you
        it's impossible to kill me.
                I've been gone.

GIRLS WANTED (PAINT ME)

Thin.

Hipless.

Light (weight).

Lighter (makeup).

Lightest (skin).

Diverse.

Give me hungry but approachable.

Diverse.

One-tenth (percent color).

Diverse.

Check & checkmate.

Got them.

Tricked them good.

Dark.

Crafty villain.

The friend that snapped the marriage.

The angry one.

No dark Black pixie dream girl.

No dark Black scientist.

Makes the lighting too tricky.

SPOTLIGHT: PERFORMANCE ON BROKEN TOE

It broke on stage
while I was pirouetting
the Black swan in red pointe shoes
               & I thought first of the lighter
that my instructor held under my
leg in practice to hoist strength
               into it, so I kept dancing—
dancing like the sky asking,
        Why do mountaintops poke so close?
Like feathers falling gently
in a sleeping city, god is a brown blanket
I sometimes sleep on, like the wind saying,
        These damn mountains keep blocking my road.
I contorted like the shadows
of gazelles jumping in African sunsets
manic dancers, a lion trailing close behind—
        so one is always dying & somewhere
it's always raining & the rain is
always humming, life *is a baptism of*
               wingless birds of shattered bones—
RUN Black girl, even if it is on ten broken toes.

You can't un-hem the <u>S</u>in.
You can't re-tilt the tale
to resurrect the dead.

You see, it's difficult
to re-skin a soul
already un-bodied.

Honey, love, sugar pie
it's all coming for you—
aunties say, *hush up,*
thicken your bones
feast when you can because
at the root, it won't be fair.

The way they will try to kill you
won't be fair.

FOR BLACK KIDS BUILDING UP THEIR BONES

A sign of summer the red strawberries on both of your knees white salt on the upper lip. Old mattress under third-story windows. Jumping spirit first, one at a time, like wingless Black doves.

Close the back door loves your dreams are falling out into the streets lock it tight. Keep the key in your front pocket, remember its weight don't let nobody touch it. Don't let nobody steal it, don't let nobody touch the growing bones of your thoughts. Push them till they break baby.

In the District the night milks out another awful moon. The lost boys wear the city streetlights like capes, they shoot blanks into the sky with silver toy guns & the girls are busy swaying the ancestry off their hips, working the kinks out of their sheep hair wringing the life out of their roots.

Last night the moonlight shot your cousin dead, shot your brother dead shot your shadow dead but the gun gets away. This city is slick as grease. You can dream until the stars become your eyes, you can pray until the night is laced up tight. There will still be splatters of red, of strawberries, of summers in the city too saturated with color.

You learned as children between the sidewalk & the curb to double-dutch quickly dodging the cutting ropes, making your feet tap till they lost their breath. Just keep jumping with splinters in your shins. Push them till they break baby.

Black butterfly you keep falling into yourself, build a skeleton out of elephant tusk & forgotten sidewalks, rib cage first. I see you kneeling at the foot of your bed, you're losing yourself like sand through fingers, a desert is forming at your base.

You are not the hands that sell the powder the venom that makes things shake, that is your brother. The electric bill is overdue. Night is cold. Bones are tired. Job is dirty. Push them till they break baby.

Baby girl's a blackbird, baby boy's her shadow, together you are the melody that makes the city lights shake to a beat sporadic & off-key. Together you erupt into a music of red flames burn yourselves hollow. Be the Black Phoenix.

This is a song for Black kids who dance slow & deliberate in the belly of the city, where the lights block out the stars. The map is missing, the Little Dipper is empty the North Star is growing old & blind. Push them till they break baby.

Red tears, you have no time to fall wipe your face before you leave. Loud shouts don't make sounds, hush them into silence. Push them till they shatter baby push them till they break. Remake.

Card Two

THE EMPRESS WITH A WHIP

femdom: says queen me

wait. stay. good good, hush, listen

now, slow—dismantle

TROUBLE

Noun: I had <u>trouble</u> unlocking
              he kept ringing at the door.

                      Adjective: My body was prepared for <u>*trouble*</u>*some times.*

                                        Verb: He punctured through.
                                            He <u>trouble</u>d me.

Colloquial: She <u>trouble</u>.
                  Not the good good kind.

Poem: {Safe Word (Ball-Change)}

<u>Trouble</u>: glare it in the eye.
Eye sockets shift—looking?
Looking lost & cry, hard cry
crystal diamonds <u>trouble</u>d & flowing down
downhill over cheekbones, off the face.

Face forward click—
click jailhouse photo
photons spark eleven.
11 guilty men line up.

Up ahead, <u>trouble</u>, they will find
                finder dead
                    dead drop
                        drop dead?

                            Dead. Gone.

FRAGMENTS OF DREAMS LEFT TO CHAR AT THE BOTTOM OF THE POT

You have to learn to get up from the table when love's no longer being served.

—*NINA SIMONE*

Dream I.

> Tuck yourself back in.
> It's not worth rebreaking
> just to heal back wrong.

Dream II.

Empty spaces in your bed collect dying languages
from the tongues you have conquered.

Dream III.

I hear god is busy,
wars keep rolling on but—
my saints have given up on me again.
They say I have joined another team.

Dream IV.

In the city of brown silk, a priest weaves prayers—
hauls them in his little red wheelbarrow to the well.
Drops each one in like printed evidence
that must be concealed.

Dream V.

My footsteps seem heavy in cathedral halls,
            would you have me dance soft instead?
I didn't follow the rules, I brought my dripping
ice cream with me—my hands are filthy.
Marked guilty.

Dream VI.

Blame Fingerprints:
            for leaving distinct dents
on all the lives they have touched,
on all the lives they are touching.

As for the lives they will soon bruise,
blame rain for washing away S̲in.

                                        Dream VII.

                        I clean dad's closet for Father's Day
                        & find receipts tumbling out of drawers,
                        inside shoes, falling from pockets.

                        Dates: 1994, 1999 & 2010,
                        evidence, just in case,
                        of his comings & goings—
                        preparation for false charges.
                        Marked guilty.

Dream VIII.

I grew up liking horses & everyone said,
your great-great-grandfather was a stable hand,
was killed by one swift blow to the head.
Stay away from horses.

As if his fate of dying
via hoof can be passed down
in my DNA, like dimples or eye color.

Dream IX.

You can't touch anything without reaction—
think how the snow gives way to angels.
Fire can only feel by consuming.
        A storm moves like a shawl
        around the shoreline's shoulders.
A fire cackles & you don't know
if it is from inside or outside your body.
        If you're afraid—(write it)
grit your teeth, they'll kill you either way, you know.

SOUTHERN GOTHIC (COME SIT)

Our meal begins at a pine table surrounded by finely dressed haunts.
      The table wears a black cloth, to hide the blood in its veins.

One white man at the head of the table with a loaded gun passes
      the bread but charred & oozing something vile & ruddy red.

He shoots one of us between the eyes, reloads & sends the bread back.
      So, we recoil & try again, sitting up straighter.

It starts with we could have been anything, day-weavers or exotic holy food.
      We could have been blessed—devoured in riot, & easily reborn.

It starts with a ghost, who thinks it is flesh. This time at a cedar table saying:
      I received so many flowers I could no longer smell death on myself.

Stage left enters boy—first name Wolf—who has never heard rain. He swears
      the cypress rain-stick sounds like falling stars. Which of course mimics rain.

The haunt who knows nothing of death thinks that death feels like living.
      Which should be inaccurate. Which should be a lie.

The deck is guillotined; the tap dancer moving over the puddle also sounds like stars—
      & rain, batons cracking Black heads & tiny heads knocking the floor.

Tea appears when it starts raining bodies. When everyone is stuffed, which should
      be impossible because food falls through our hazy guts to the floor.

We pretend to eat but keep nothing—so <u>thick</u>-less we drift.
      So, we float, shuffle seats & begin again.

Hate is a concept that only love can understand.
      Which is absurd; you don't need a partner to dance.

The Black boy haunt at the end of the table has a bullet lodged in his stomach—
    the hole still aches freshly, wine seeps from it rudely.

The man with a gun claims he will shoot anything—dead or alive.
    He aims between our eyes & shoots us each again.

Stop searching. There is no trail to this grave—death comes
    like vultures promised meat. The crime devoured before it is seen.

The bullet in my head cries like love—without control.
Like a corpse decays like laughter—without a care for time.

DUTCH DOOR (1940)

In the south, the door is kept closed
at the bottom, sometimes even with
a towel kissing the seam where light
crawls in, to keep out those wretched
legless things the bible calls snakes.

The top is swung open, for Mama or Grammy
to trace, with eyes rimmed bloodshot,
the roots of trees that double age them
in the front yard.
       Mama will say, hands stained
from crushing for strawberry jam,
the roots say the tomatoes
               will freeze off the vines tonight.
She'll say it always thinking of the body she witnessed
at six, swinging heavy in a Poplar Tree before
the half-burnt rope untwined & the body dropped.

Papa huffs, folding the newspaper
with hands grafted with a thousand Mississippi
scars from working on other people's farms.
It's not far to the barn & Papa finds
an old, hay-gouged blanket to tuck
in the tomatoes thriving on his land.

Mama says, *the roots like to know*
       you love them. Living things can't live with no love.
As if it is not about the blanket
but the act of tucking, of whispering,
       Y'all stay warm now, you hear.

So, Papa says, *y'all stay warm now, you hear,*
& Grammy watches with hands calloused enough
to push hot pans back into the oven
without wince or blister.

Mama wipes her fingers roughly
on the front of her red apron,
watching her husband tuck in the red tomatoes,
watching dusk slice a reddish line in the sky.
       Even her children, reddened from playing
in clay soil all day & scabby from picking
& itching mosquito bites now bleeding.
Mama calls her babies in—
      their eyes bright from
          double-dutching over fireflies.

Mama closes the window part of the door—
      locks it tight knowing in the south,
night fogs in heavy & hungry for old ways.
She bathes her children in lantern light,
the water tints red from dirt,
          clay, scabs.

Mama says,
    do we all inherit
blood that stays outside the body?
What god makes things this way?

BLACK GODDESS WAS BUILT

get this, a goddess
        space-marsh birthed
with hands larger than
the underbelly of the universe
spit sparkles from her
lipstick mouth
        onto the canvas.

                        that's why our eyes are clear-sighted

get this, a goddess
        with an ass as round as two Plutos
lassoed together twerks a ripple in time.

                        that's called déjà vu, honey

get this, a goddess empty as the chamber
        of a fired gun can't stop a bullet
'cause god made it so.

                        that's called jealousy

get this, a goddess was pissed,
squeezed the life out of
a black hole so she was renamed: plague—
        which just means
                too wild to rule, too feared to worship.
Which really means
        afraid of punishment deserved.

EULOGY FOR BLOOD LEFT BEHIND

I.

This haven, mossed & quaint, is not heaven—
            in the summer it sleets Black doves,
I swear the plank it pours them.

A muted choir gurgles,
beneath the mud near the Black Ash Tree
            where snakes with lies stuffed down
their endless throats hang, hooked
& ready.

            The toes of the low marsh drain
& lilies pop up each *flee* season—
headstones for the bodies consumed.

II.

As a haunt
I am skinless, <u>thick</u>-less
muddied, naked & mapped.

The dipper carved into
forearm bone.

Not humbled, I am soaring.
Not missed, I am dead.

III.

I hear White Mountains have left
        their peaks & valleys have taken the high road.
Hot springs have drained themselves of heat
& water, being water, still claims to clean—to purify.

The marsh being the marsh holds bodies—its prey—
under rocks & between the fingers of twigs.

Me being a haunt, I offer myself.

Stories declare my Black naked body baptizes water.
        My breasts can mask the Sin on many things, but not this.
I wasn't built to only be tugged to the guillotine.

BLACK WITCH MOTH

(Ascalapha odorata)

They think it's the moonbeams—
    iridescent, irresistible, asking for irresponsibility.
Honey, the moon has never been white.

Its hopeless swagger—
a skip to the inevitable. It is better to jump
than be pushed off the plank.

    More moth saying: *I'll kill myself before I let you touch me.*
        I am a master of rebirth.
    More light saying: *We got them, we slaughtered them.*

THERE ARE MANY CHURCHES

They said, *honey, there are crimson roses*

                    spilling from

                              my ears,

                                   my nose,

                                        my mouth

                                             it hurts,

                                                  help,

                                                       don't stop.

She said—*(. . .)*

          (. . .)

                    (. . .)

                         (. . .)

                              (. . .)

                                   (. . .)

                                        (. . .).

She didn't say anything,

just kept a steady pace on the prayer

just tightened the leash

& listened for the crescendo

the hymn hung gentle on the wind.

WAP (THE WHOLE DAMN MEAL)

A feast. Not the thanksgiving kind—
          create a new holiday,
'cause I don't celebrate with Sins.
I am vaster than turkey
& fixins & lies
& dust mites
eating darker letters
in history books.

I am water.
Not the southern marsh,
        or the Mississippi still digesting bones.
Not like the middle ocean, trading Black bodies—
more like the Congo, Zambezi & Niger combined (somehow).

I am Black & Woman which means
        my pain levels are higher.
                My death rate is higher.
                        My (almost) death days higher.
                                Most likely for things unwanted.

A priest told me,
the hue of death strangles your shadow.

I said, *that's quite a fit*
        an impressive drip
                don't you think?

See, 'cause I am a witch & a psalm—
red snakes have traveled down my throat
                    sprouted from my hair follicles.

I was feasted on then un-blessed—
                    Mami Wata wading in the Mississippi.

TWO-HEADED SNAKE

if you & one other
  come upon one—
& just dead or nearly
& if you happen to have gloves
  in that dash compartment
  or between the front seats
& if (somehow) you have a lighter
  that has been handled
  by a preacher who pretends
  not to smoke, but goes
  to the graveyard to huff away

if you have these tools
& it happens to be
  the night before
  a full moon
& the two-headed snake was moving
  east toward hell's first gate
& if one of you grabs it
  by its endless tail
& holds it taut
& the other hovers
  the lighter below the belly
  for no more than a minute
  no less than 55 seconds

you'll see them
legs tiny & stump-like

& don't look for long
   those legs are hell-bound
   leave it where you found it

& burn the gloves
& bury the lighter
   under a grave with an *S*-starting name
   <u>S</u>am, <u>S</u>usan, <u>S</u>inner . . .

& don't (for christ's sake) position a camera
   to witness the dead thing animate
   twisting & withering
   until spikes & claws form
& it digs through the center
of the earth on its way
to the other side
dis-ease ripe
in its belly
fertilizing
the soil.

EMPRESS WITH A MAGIC TRICK

a girl with blood in her hands
        bats on her lashes
walks into a bar, lays an egg right in her chair
says, *scrambled hard*—& because she is more air than body
the bartender obeys

different girl this time with diamonds
        for eyes, twigs bundled &
stuffed into the stubs of her wrists
says, *tell me a tall tale*—& because she has gems
        they want them
men fall over themselves to talk
                    they tell her about the year
                      the white horse came,

the harvest forgot to bloom
all the fathers lived; every mother died
all the babies grew fat

same girl cries literally cries her eyes out
        & because her jewels are gone the men leave richer

fresh with blindness she says, *I can't find my way*—
        & because she is new to the simple feel of the world
        she is led somewhere the opposite of home

a girl with shipwreck in her hair
       & bullet holes for dimples walks into a bar
slaps her leather gloves on the counter
says, *god did not send me* & because she says it
       like an invitation
she might be asking for it

men try to touch her
       she laughs, gurgles a flood
right out of her crimson mouth
& because she is more vessel than body
she keeps her arc of a tongue to herself
       everyone drowns & she struts out

Card Three

fasten up the doors

logic the logiclessness

gotta silence sit

THICK (AGAIN)

Noun: His-story is <u>thick</u>ness.

           Adjective: <u>Thick</u> retellings, stories <u>thick</u> with rot.

                    Adverb: <u>Thick</u>ly a boot stomps
                              on a Black face.
                         They <u>thick</u>ly hate us.

Colloquial: <u>Thick</u> for what?

Poem: {Mud City (Ball-Change)}

The girls make <u>thick</u> mud-packed snowballs—
                    ballers of the dirt yard.
Yards & yards of anthills,
        hillbilly heaven, they call it, with its dust.
Dusty hidden backroads & <u>thick</u> rusty sun
sunshining hard on the back.

Back porch of the house—
house-haint lives & inside the house
                (house-inside yourself)
self-proclaimed queen of mud.

Mud city; ant heaven.
(Heaven is not here in this mud.)
Muddy-red; cradling lost bones.

DUPLEX (DID NOT RUN FAST ENOUGH)

Be still, the sunshine has been known to shoot
the skin of those who are <u>thick</u> with pigment.

The skin of those who are <u>thick</u> with pigment,
to the touch, is smoother than a bleached crime scene.

To the touch, is smoother than a cleaned crime scene,
blood hidden in cranberry juice bottles, bones in floor-bellies.

Blood hidden in cranberry juice bottles, bones in floor-bellies
hushed & forgotten for years, until there is a water leak.

Bones hushed & forgotten for years, until there is a water leak.
The floors are forced inside out—exposing—femur, a right pinky bone.

The floors are forced inside out—exposing a femur, a right pinky bone,
a skull with a note stuffed between the white-bright teeth.

A skull with a note stuffed between the white-bright teeth,
  Went out at day, the (white-washed) sunshine got me good.

HIPBONES

It's foggy inside
because of the windows
conversed all moontime with ghosts
which cling, a heavy dew, to the panes
                    blocking the sunbeams.

                              Inside I deathed another
                              Sin-stuffed Icarus saying,
                              at least I did not fracture you
                                        enough to steal your soul.

                    Panting beside me he says,
                    all the ghost stories are about you
                    slurping silver linings like spaghetti.

& on cue, handprints appear
on the foggy window.
& he runs for the front door
that is already hotter than hell.

                         He begs,
                    you are trouble,
                    who sent you?

Who else would send me
but myself.

SOUTHERN LOVE STORY ONE: CALL ME THE FIRST HORSE-WOMAN

I make a feast for dinner. Sitting across the table like chess pieces, I am bridled.
I don't understand this game how am I all four horse-pieces & you none?
    I frown, but my eyebrows smile. You gobble supper down like a snack,
chuck on a coat with silver trim, which means you are going somewhere special
    without me again.

Then comes night, hours stack precariously, stretched out thin
& slow—like atoms across dark matter. The apparitions I collect
    & pay with lust await you by the front door.
I lie in bed with a white sheet pulled over my head.
Empty as a drought; alone as a webbed window.

I warn you, the next day, as I line the house with the same plastic
    you rolled out for me—I say, *I have an idea, death moth.*
Run away as fast as you can—It's not enough just to want it.
Don't think you hear me. Your flimsy wings crumple instead of spread.

You drink a Blue Moon as I slap on plastic gloves, whipping my tongue saying,
    I have more cracks than a map of California fault lines—
you are my San Andreas. Your fault of a mouth pushes against mine
like it belongs to you, but lines with seams always break.

With a knife I practice cutting branches from the Christmas tree because
    December is a stormy season; we always take six steps backward,
finding ourselves in the place we were supposed to leave.

Six beers in & passed out I straddle you like a horse. It is important to be precise—
        you took my heart years ago, placed it right on top of yours.
The seam opens easily, like a mouth with no teeth to protect it.

My heart beats out of tune above yours. I whisper, *we are leaving,*
        we are slamming the door; we were always just passing through.
I know it knows I am lying. I know it knows what I mean.

I replace my own organ then grasp the one underneath. I have to pull hard
        before it plucks out like a stubborn flower. I find a jar
with daisies—I am not so cruel. I won't keep something that is not mine
        inside me. I bury your heart, with the white horse-piece, under the willow,
with enough blood to last a year.

You wake breathless. I have cleaned & changed. I say, *hush, I have a secret,*
        death moth. You will fall in & out of night with me.
I make a snack for dinner; fullhearted, my hips are happy to be swaying again.

SOUTHERN LOVE STORY TWO: WE HAVE ALL SINNED

Tiny & pearl-white & almost innocent—it did not take long
       for horns to grow, resembling milk teeth. Next—a tail, a red nub
sprouting in the basin of your back. I ask you to waltz & your nails
claw at my sides.

I file the claws down, but they sprout furious as arrows overnight.
       Your hands now weapons—I sleep in the guest bedroom.

Sometimes I check on your heart, buried under the willow,
with the white horse-piece, in the jar filled with blood. Your heart, always needy,
       devoured the blood faster than anticipated. I slice my wrist
& offer some of mine. The heart without a body grows black,
so I add vinegar so the organ will keep.

Your nails grow slower, we see someone about the tail,
       the horns we file down weekly. Unfortunately, you develop
a hop—both rabbit & strangely daemon-like. You want to play chess,
but four horse-pieces have galloped off.

In October, the willow's leaves shift to a ghastly red. At night the hue reflects
       the moon & turns our house crimson. I drag my body from
bed & pad across the yard. The jar has sunk deeper into the earth.

I raise the jar to the moonlight. Your heart has grown veins
       that reach toward the cap twisting.
I apply duct tape to keep the beast inside.

Thanksgiving, everything speeds up. Your tail is now near your knees.
      You have to hide it in one pant leg for work. You take to wearing hats
to cover the horns bursting from behind your ears.

I know I should put the heart back; living things should live inside living things,
      but I like you like this. Strange & ragged like me.
With the cold, a crack inches up the willow & I worry it will split in two.

One day you insist on cutting my hair. Black & ravenous,
      it turns you on too much,
& because of your claws we can't screw so, it has to go.

Like Samson, my legs grow weaker. Light things become lead in my arms.
      You sew my hair into your jacket with silver trim
& somehow become taller.

You still leave, but not till midnight, when it is easier to hide the horns.
Then I haul out the albums of the years before. I notice the points
      of my nails, the shadows of horns under my hair.

I see the apple, meant for our four horses. The apple I chewed
      & kissed into your mouth humming, *you'll like it, you'll like it*, & you do like it,
& we do love it, until, of course, we don't & we burn.

paradise is a world where everything
is a sanctuary & nothing is a gun.
—*DANEZ SMITH*

The spider is first.
I can hardly feel the legs
on my skin, like a stitch in a Sin.

Like a stitch looped from lip
to lip & tightened.

I like a Sin.
The small kind.

Hands are fine
if they are breeze—
hovering, plane-like,
closer only when begged.

I like a Sin. The forgivable kind.
The bloodless kind.

Anger starts as a tickle.
Like a mosquito
that kisses, then itches, then scars.

I like a scar if it stays closed

but when you die in the streets
you are moved to a morgue.

The wound is widened
to stitch in a note:
bullet shot officer innocent,
Black &
too imposing.

Dead skin is stitched back together
—like a <u>S</u>in.

That's not a scar.
The flesh won't knit
back together
with forgiveness.

THE HOUSE THAT DRIPS

Blood but not because of haunts,
because a man was shot, on the second floor
& the blood soaked into the softness
of the wood.

& they say the body stayed there
unfound for so long that first skin
fell off like fish scales.

At some point wild things got into the house.
The coroner says, *the bite marks scraping*
prayers on the bones are certainly not human
they are coyote born.
In his notes he added, *perhaps a three-toothed bear*
pitchforked, made the rib cage give.

We Hoodoo knew it was Satan,
white with fury,
            but we nodded anyway.

There were only bones there
when they found him.
            His soul had long left the room,
but strange fire burned in the corner
that could not put it out—
not with water, nor ice.

They brought a priest,
who brought a virgin,
who called a Conjurer,
who only came because
the bones were Black—
          they were just bones but she knew.
She told her ancestors
& the fire dimmed
& ashed out.

But the blood stayed.
When it storms, the roof—
now decomposed—lets in ruddy rain.

They called the house America.
Deemed it unlivable—
paid a Conjurer to sink it
into the ground.

Built a new house on top,
sturdy walls & roof,
but when it rains—
still deluge.
Still blood.

AMERICAN FABLE

You woke up dead,
intention gone wolf,
a tongue of fraying ribbon,
       it licked its lips & nipped.

Fall into the wind, let it support
       the soles of your feet.
Forgotten every psalm? Go make love,
whisper. Call it prayer. Braid your hair
grow it out until it locs, call yourself messiah,
       who's to say you're not?

In an orange shirt
       you resemble a phoenix strutting
porch rails, quilting the sun out of the sky.

Mouth hopeless. Drowned—soaked from clothes
to bone.

Morning rituals (wash, brush, medicate), a life stares you down
       don't scare easy, don't throw stones.

There are things you will pick up just to see how easily you can drop them.

There are things you will misplace
       (birth bones, innocent bodies, bullet wounds, milk teeth).

NOT EVEN A NINA SIMONE HYMN CAN PERFORM MAGIC TRICKS

Tires brake on a velvet road so there is not a screech, but rather a rustle like fall leaves humping. A body flies through waterfall windows, so there is no shattering just splattering & a soft land that hardly knocks the wind from caged lungs. When it is all said & done, you can easily resurrect, hair drenched & walk back to the car drowning in the smoke of Nina Simone tones with only a bruise growing on your shoulder blade like a birthmark, X-marking the spot for you—later.

Later, it will be moonless & Nina won't be playing, so nothing is velvet & the window is a window that if broken will shatter knives & lies. This time it's not a crash, it's a pull-over for a taillight that you forgot to get fixed. It's a pull-over for an air freshener that keeps the weed smell at bay. It's a pull-over & it's a man in a uniform that is anything but velvet that holds your voice in the eight-foot-deep coffin of his mouth for—later.

Later, there is a coffin with your limpness inside being lowered into the ground because you reached for a registration & in the moonless night your hand was so dark the uniform mistook it for a gun. & because he knew you had <u>trouble</u> in your skin, he shot once into your shoulder blade making you fall forward hitting play & Nina turned on (accidentally). The bullet didn't want to be in your body it wanted to be in the velvet air holding Nina's voice, so it went all the way through (apologizing on the exit) kissing every organ, begging them to heal—later.

Later the mortician played Nina while sewing closed the tiny entry wound & screaming exit hole. Later they play Nina Simone while showing photos on a projector screen. People hold fistfuls of tears. You can't hold a fistful of tears. You can't hold thousands of names—they fall through your fingers <u>S</u>infully softly like the sound of a velvet voice—crumbling on the asphalt—like a miracle making a full stop, the Red Sea crashing without apology.

THISTLE AT (ANOTHER) FUNERAL

It rains
        & believers sing,
& my tie a purple thistle,
a silken weight, flat between
my breast.

Unrelenting—each psalm
more weight—my ribs screech.

My mind races to some dirt road
        where darkness
folds into darkness—where I ride a crazed
Pegasus raises dust. Where I straddle time
& beg her to deliver the soul back to the body.

But I am here, Me, here, hiding—
in the pews as silent as a seahorse—
        except for the breaking.

They play Nina Simone & close it,
snap you into a velvet heaven
        in your lavender tie—more weight.

But why am I telling you this?
        Why am I praying to the silent cross (again)?

GHOST MOTH

(Thysania agrippina)

Naturalist tried to catch them by showering pellets—
      strangely elusive they hardly fell like snow
   or sleet, or ice, or medium-sized hail from the sky.

They flew, just darty enough, reached just high enough,
      seduced the space between tree branches just enough.

The truth is their bodies are so thin compared to their wings.
    By shrinking themselves for years the bullets just miss
their Black souls—naturalists called them witches or ghosts.
             'Cause anything that dodges death that much
                  ain't all human, which is also why
             naturalists don't mind killing them.

Y'ALL CAN PRAY TOO MUCH (PESTILENCE STEPS OUT)

An epidemic of prayers
   tugged carefully from the mouth
of an auntie in a swampy backwoods pew
somewhere on the line between Virginia
& North Carolina have
   for no reason apparent
up & left their offering dish—
huddled closer together than recommended
with their begging, they plan to mutiny the skin of the sky
which is pulled thinner than cellophane
over the roundness of an expanding balloon
which is to say,
   shit here is about to get real.

In retaliation, the sky epidemic'ed rain as salty
   as the saline solution injected
as a placebo into veins of the hopeful who said,
I don't want to haunt shadows,
   I'll try anything.
     Please, help me.

Tell me, what is the thought
   of saving without the act?
In these dry times, some will claim
thoughts & prayers are a mercy
which is to say,
   the rain doesn't fall
     right anymore.
      Salt slithered in.

Science: salt shifts unnoticed into cells
unweaving DNA. Drying us out.
Doesn't matter where the salt came from
it's everywhere now, it eats through borders.

Then again, what is an epidemic
but a magic trick?
A virus slaps on a goofy mask
with a mustache & says,
I promise this time will be different,
   let me in. It's cold,
     it's raining, honey, let me in.

A flaw in our crafting: we were birthed hungry,
   born so thirsty we rise at dawn
to wolfishly lick dew from flower petals.
So, we open,

    open,

    open . . .
every cell—

   not even god could have expected
it to be this easy to crack us. Almost insulting,
somethings dirt-sprung from infinite hands
are so easy to grind to dust.

Pastors in pulpits said,
This here, this right here is the devil's work.
  It came here because we have <u>*Sinned.*</u>
   The Black woman has <u>*Sinned*</u> *most of all.*
Pray more, louder, vaster, pray lustfully . . .

You see, because of the expensive salt encased
in each raindrop, everything is dampened,
but dehydrated because there are so many prayers
god can't hear anything through the static.

Problems require solutions,
so a tool is invented that can remove
salt from each droplet for a dollar,
            but a billion drops per square mile,
                    a billion raindrops per square mile,
that is to say,
the rain is too expensive a problem
for money to afford.

So, it rains, it monsoons,
everything is dampened—
quenched for a moonrise
then shrivels up,
dies.

Even the epidemic.

Which is to say,
            thoughts & prayers.

Card Four

THE DEVIL'S SISTER (upright)

it's me, come back strong

me, resurrected myself

bribed the ferryman good

TROUBLE (AGAIN)

Noun: I am <u>trouble</u>.

Adjective: I am <u>trouble</u>some.

Verb: Watch me <u>trouble</u> away.

Colloquial: <u>Thick</u> with <u>trouble</u>.

Poem: {Spell/Psalm}
a southern daughter three times over.
      i am <u>thick</u> with <u>trouble</u>—
i turned on the lantern
then burned it all down.

WASHINGTON DC BURNING

Tonight, DC is burning.
The sunset on the capital casts
a shadow that spills like a boiling flood
down the hill, into the city, curdling
the blood in people's veins.

& the mermaids in the Potomac boil
& shriek & that's how we know
they are there.

& the shriek of the bullet
is how we know a recently
un-bodied Black
haunt hangs near.

These are things we know now
          so we walk different.

Some are not of this shapeless
          flee season that stretches 365 days
running through the streets punishing.

Careful: when cornered, I have seen shadow easily demolish
          things that hide in the sun.

THAT'S NOT A SCAR: MUSEUM EXHIBIT (IN MY MIND)

Exhibit I.

In Vietnam, Black boys
were told to scorch huts
next to white boys
who preferred burning crosses
       in cornfields back home.

Exhibit II.

In the season of diamonds
it rained blood arms & legs.
People still bought them,
    weighed & washed them.

Exhibit III.

City boys carry guns
because the police carry guns.
Your death was not televised
so it never happened.
& every Sunday has been bloody
since I don't remember.

Exhibit IV.

History is bony figures, bloody knuckles
& guttural moans fall out of the bookshelf.
Drag themselves across the wooden
    planks leaving stains, living stains.

Exhibit V.

When the story snuggles in
like a pup in your lap, commit the trill
to memory, borrow the marrow.
It's heavy to carry it, decaying.

Let's try again. A nightmare walks up
behind you? Side-step & watch it zombie along
hoping to be found.

Exhibit VI.

The boy with brown eyes
& full lips walked to a party
was dying to be kissed.
He never felt the blow that killed him.
You never feel the blow that kills you.

Exhibit VII.

A Black woman with a broken leg
a fractured arm, is told to dance
or, with a snap of the fingers,
humanity dies—
        but she doesn't remember how to dance,
how to be filled with air, thoughtless—free.
It all ends because of *them*, not her.

ABRACADABRA

from the Aramaic languages, meaning I will create as I speak

I.

Selma has a bug-laced cocktail, ciphers blood
into her fish tank, even adopts frogs.
     She turns off all her lights to study bleakness.
She thinks that marking doors,
     the intention of sacrifice will be enough.

II.

     Angry battalions
swing the time as 3, 2, 1.

There is no godmother—
     so we kneel for god.

Prayer rubs soft, gives way to clouds—
     skulls crack & crack.

The prettiest girl, Selma,
wears her feet proudly.
     Leaking with blisters
& beaten so badly
watermark bruises blossom.
     Each toe turns to coal.

III.

Selma carries herself home
in her own cupped palms.

Her spirit leaks through the gaps
leaving a trail, an arrow pointing
to her front door.

She places herself on the kitchen table
pours Epsom salts, soaks, waits—
       opens her bible
adds *Sunday* to the plagues,
steps out her house.

EXQUISITE CORPSE (AMERICA'S HOUSE)

I would like to be clear
       because clarity, of late, has become a joke
shuffled & re-decked & counted
& sniffed & swished around in dry mouths
       but never eaten.

                         Honey, you must eat to taste.

I am tired, tired of
       sticky & <u>S</u>inful
with rot blood moons.
I am bored with the sun
& bone-white sidewalks graffitied red.

The rules have been botched,
how can I hide when you don't even count?
       I can't breathe, I can't keep warm in hoodies,
I can't stand on sidewalks, *I can't breathe*
       I can't, I can't breathe
under this weight.

              A litany of the brutality of forgetfulness.

Let's glide on the edge of disaster /
           paper cut hard / pick scabs too early /
break knuckles on brick /
'cause pain has become a habit.

        How does forgetting become a nation's favorite hobby?

I can't breathe /
       handcuffed / shackled?
I can't breathe /
       sidewalk / lashing.

Let me be clear: a ghost can't write a ghost story.

America the dark circles
under your eyes
      are carrying the weight
of funeral drums.
Give them a break.
      Eat.
Learn the art of harvest—
properly tend to the things behind you.

Let me be clear: this is a threat, *HANDS UP.*

Eat from the plate
you so carefully assembled.
Taste the ash, the blood, that strange scrape
of teeth on teeth, that hint of molten metal.

Let me be clear: this is a feast
      lick your S̲in-filled plate
leave nothing behind, remember it all.

Don't forget to clean the bone.

DAMN, AMERICA

ate my breath away
   like a whale eats krill
   more gobble than bite
more banquet than meal

     all edges & (untranslated) smoke signals
     shadowing themselves into crooked hooks
      & mallets

        into hooded figures prettifying in white

America: submissive:
takes a beating: pants
   begs for more

    let's negotiate a safe word
     stop would be best

         each fib a needle packed
          into the pores
        of a nation raising them
          scarification
       dotting out a warning on flesh
         in pimpled braille

facts did not line up
        they were politely asked to move
        to the back
more facts misbehaved
        & thus were strung up
                like *strange fruit*

                tasteless as cold toast
                loveless like broken sex

                        voice: prickly as pineapple skin
                                alleged: true
                          fake news: truest god

Damn, America, you slink
sightless: backward-footed
        twisted at the ankle & pinched at the wrist

                hands: everywhere
                hands: in every pot

                                coin flips
                  heads up: protest: ants swarming
                heads cut off: protest: flowers planted

America darling
        your mother-tongue is hate
        it is easy to slip back into
a dress that is only a little too small

America? I can't hear you
you were there
for the conception
parties flicking & licking
each other on the ear

there for the birth
(rhetoric-sainted teeth)

don't applaud yourself
for hunkering down
for delivering the placenta

that is your job
to fix it
to handle things you craft

your voice cracks
take this tea
loosen the noose
spit out the hard
syllabus of your name
find the softness again

lure the men out of the city
into your dark valley

crush them between your thighs
like nuts cracked at Christmas

                                                    we have been
                                                over this before

breathe from
the diaphragm

                    louder this time
                             try again
                        push it out—
                        fully formed.

HOODOO (HOME)

It is strangely silent.
The way the woods are quiet,
but teeming with eyes.

By the third month—
small sounds, missing forks,
        water faucets making an ocean of the first floor,
hangers twist into nooses—or are they hearts?

A woman with three fingers and one eye tells me:
        the dead like living things.

I grow trees, plant flowers—
offerings of life, unsure if it is a gift
or a torment.

Afraid of stillness, I pace a line from door to window.
        I study movement in all things—daisies twist
        their necks for the sun. The air-conditioning system
        aspires to be an opera singer. Shadows grow taller
        eating up my wooden floors.

Then it happens—
        I start to worry if the light in the kitchen
does not flicker on right as I fall asleep,
drawing attention to the lack of consciousness in the room.
        Proof that even the dead hate
being the only ones awake. So I wake.

THE EULOGY FOR SOLITUDE & F'S TO GIVE

I know something about
how this thing called time dissolves
into misplaced f's to give & I pace for
sleep, which is hiding wide-eyed in a cemetery
near a grave I can't visit.

The creak in the fourth floorboard is planning
against my footsteps, which lead me upstairs
to my shower where I have grown accustomed
to having conversations on water, with water—
       drips off the tin roof of my mouth.

Outside it is sleeting Black doves (again), hailing Black ribbons (again)—
       Black laced gloves, Black people in a church,
Black bodies rinsed of blood & placed into caskets.

GOOD-GOODBYE

i think you are crying
it's hard to tell
with the rain & wind
& everyone dressed
from toe to crown in black

you push your damp hair
from your face screaming
into the unforgiving air
  you are nothing now
    but a haunted house

i've heard this before
it's true
  it's foggy inside me
when i open my mouth
clouds tumble out

i think i am dead
  i think i've gone ghost

i walk elsewhere
i leave soggy & barefoot
roots bubbling from the soil
leading me to the end or the start

don't follow me
  please (i am old) don't follow me
    this is a good-goodbye.

I WON'T LET ANYONE (BLACK) DIE ALONE

When you die, I'll wear you like invisibility
keep you like a phantom limb. I'll cast spells
on my skin, leaving enough braille
to remember what rot blurs.

Why are we trained to cut red strings, to shake
off pain so fast? Why am I still sitting here,
rocking between straight tie business meetings
& strip naked runaway wolf-child?

Body & soul feasting at opposite ends
of the table—realms apart. Legs crossed
like kindergarten, like bowed cherry stems.

I'll beg your ghost back, I'll say:
let's pass moths between our mouths,
build a town of pumpkins & Christmas trees.

I'll maneuver around your shadow
during morning rituals & I'll have to remember
to place you in the ground before work.

Excessive fancy is a prescription. They'll cram me
with pills, but I won't stop watering you
& if drums are welcome in every song
why not love in every poem?

I'd love you: present tense & remember
how you used to open me each morning,
astonished that the night could change a body so much.

I will build a something, with chewed paper for legs
& kite arms, to fly,
to slow dance furious in the sky with you while I sleep.
I've come back strong. I won't let you die alone.

Card Five

abracadabra

Black girl paves her own way home

abracadabra

VENUS FLYTRAP

I step out of the house they say I built
with a match between my lips & gasoline
strapped like a guitar on my hip.

I have left before
            with fewer tools—a match,
no gasoline, no water.

Often just hands, sometimes just casted arm
or the hue of blue blossoming crow's feet around my eye.

This time, I forget shoes,
that is how I know—the soft soil begs
me forward, covers my scent.

            When jesus left he was barefoot.
The bible doesn't say that, but I know better.
I know you need a mother to cradle your feet.

I pour gasoline—
            a vein of fire.
The wooden teeth of the porch
snap at me, threaten me back in,
just for a moment, just for shoes—
            just so I have no mother beneath me.

My feet are already bleeding,
        hips have already forced themselves between mine,
        the fire that erupted after has burned the edges of memory.
I look back at the red shock of a door—light it up.

If I go back for shoes,
        I'll need sugar & eggs.

The door will hide itself,
the locks will turn so slow I can't hardly hear them.

The windows upstairs will be open,
but what's the point of an abundance of windows
when there are no doors?

ROAM WILD & WOLFISH (SHE WILL COME)

With flies clinging to her curls
like specks of pepper.

Skin like the underside
of a penny left
in the rain.

She will hover—
        before deciding,
grinning larger than
a mountain range
daggered teeth flashing.

She will arrive saying—
        I have been watching you
atop a white horse named Pestilence.

She will arrive—
        darker than the space
between glittering stars.
Stomach filled with gumbo
& chicken legs.

As good as the earth
        (the earth that birthed her)
& that is when they will know
they fucked up.

WHEN ICARUS WAS A WOMAN

Death:

The water was frantic, spewing at the eyes of the sky.
　　My wings, blue & magnificent, drank in foam.
The cliffs, jagged saints, had a funeral for my bones.

Church:

1. Hold out your palms like boats above the ground. When they cross to pray place a cross & build around it.
2. You will need to find a woman, a saint, with ropes for veins & a river of a mouth. Ropes for hoisting, water for movement.
3. Don't forget the nails, they should be silver, smooth & blunt. Preferably from the mouth of an Eve.
4. Salt for circles.
5. Salt around the entire church.

Resurrection:

The son is never close enough to burn.
The ghost moves all boulders.
My father only gave me one Icarus feather.
In this story, I fly wherever in hell I want.

NEOPHYTE PSALM

If I had a hymn it would sound like
Skittles spilt on the kitchen floor.
Or water inside the tin of a mouth,
but mostly like a sponge sinking.

Yellow & round, it sings about nothing
because it's busy with drowning itself.
        Bloated, filthy & full of oceans.

No one ever cares about the stuff
that needs cleaning, the layer of film
that builds up on everything.

A good scrubbing won't fix this.

Even one's insides should be brushed daily.
Except for the heart—leave it alone.
It grows smart with dirt,
        brilliant with decay.

WHEN I HEAR TALK OF THE EDGE

According to the moon waves
& the scraps of hooligan leaves
kissing the inside of my teacup
it's coming, the edge,
the literal end of ends
& (of course)
I am literally
sipping tea.

Unrelated: did you know
when a crab is dropped
(in already boiling water)
      it tries to jump out right away.

Related to the above: did you know
if a crab is dropped in cold water
& slowly (ever so slowly)
the temperature is raised
the crab will inspect
its own arm and say,
      will you look at that?
      My insides are cooking,
I think I will stay here.

All that to say,
when the apocalypse comes
to burn down *this* house
      I am not a crab.
I am the one slowly
      (ever so slowly) bringing the heat.

I AM THE FLOOD & FIRE XOXO

The cargo   in your stomach
you were supposed to   easily digest.

It never should have   sprouted fingering
its way into   your nervous system.
You kept it   because you wanted to.
You must fancy   the ache.

Like a river
    loves the rapids,
    love loves the ocean.

Like the flower
    loves the garden,
    love loves the field.

A fist is just   a closed hand.
A tornado   a pissed-off storm.

When the earth quakes   it realizes it is cracking itself—
it is supposed to be   a warning.

Intent: waves sweep your feet   fire changes matter.

It is not meant to burn or drown   it just is.

Perspective. Man: a rock.

Woman: a vessel.

Woman: a boat.

During the flood   she held man, in her stomach.

He was not a polite guest   when *she* birthed him, he forgot her name.

A hurricane   strong breeze, the wind from 4 horses' mouths.

Hello, man, Icarus,

heard a rumor there will be fire   I'll be keeping the water for myself.

SNACK

un-meditate,
fan away the circles
of smoke & un-sage
        peaceful stillness

buck-wild naked wolf child

slice through
the crisp apple orb
of calm & sit
sit with this anger
(spiteful & flickering).

army crawl the length
of a trigger finger

coil spiral inward
snake attack ready

the black widow
webbing in the window
        all eight legs tapping
don't wait up, honey,
        sweet & silent
have left the chat

I sucked them dry
        I ate them like a snack

I DON'T CARE ABOUT ICARUS

[again] i've asked god
to step off
            my neck

told him to shorten his fingers

isn't squirming a better punishment
            candle wax melted
[again] drip
drip [again]

on the gravel lane [again]
            digging for bones
to replace my own
looking for dust
            to seal my seams

i am the center
            circle [again]
surround
            naked, contorting, coaxing

i kill Icarus [again]
i bribe the sun [again]

a burnt-out match
      white flurry of wings
not forgotten

instead a boy
the color of foam
      wave eaten

not driftwood

not a brown wooden boy

with black wings
with no repeat eulogy

      a wooden boy
      is left to rot on the rocks [again]

left a warning in the sky [again]—
      I killed Icarus

i hope white men pace [again] wondering
when I will be <u>thick</u> with <u>trouble</u>—
      wondering when I will come snip their wings.

PRETTY PLEASE: CLIP MY WINGS: CAST ME OUT

If your heaven arranges itself in circles
        let me
           garden
              the lowest.
                    I chew with my mouth pasture wide
                      which means I'd rather not dine
                      with saints & my fit is too fresh
                      to mingle with saviors in rags.

                      Let me ghost here.

Cut off the tags. Arrange me prettily—
        mannequin me,
bind me in linen or tattoo me in nettle.

        Leave me with women. Smother me
           down
              down
hold me under
between the legs of air
for one Mississippi,
        two Mississippi,
        ten Mississippi,
please drown me in sky.
I promise I won't utter
              one/safe/word.

Or keep me in a copper cup,
I'll actress the grease
not thrown out.
I said, keep me nearby the stove
to witness the feast, call my name
              in famine.

Witness me like this:
The girl in the woods holding a mason jar
swimming with oatstraw's milky tops—
        saying, *I lit the lantern*
I know what hangs in your closet.

Pretty please watch me.
I'll invisible in the mundane
& report back lying only when necessary—

let me stay woke on the gossip
of the ground folk.

Let me dive deeper than the nested
network of pine tree roots.

I'll hover-hot with air
please I am too well-intentioned
for any circle below.

Too Black for anything so divine—
You see, the fact that bullets sail
instead of fall like lead
is proof enough that any god
I love is gone.

Let me get gone—
        here, hovering.

Let me ghost here forever—
        tell folks the lore of me.
        Gospel me into folklore.

THE BIRTHING OF (<u>SSSSSSSSS</u>NAKE ME)

My grandma says, *there are two births. The get born one & no more fucks to give one.* She says, *the second one is the hardest. You gotta rebreak to set it right.*

So, I arrived late (again): crafted in a cauldron from the scraps of planets & pine bark. My heart slim & <u>S</u>in-stuffed—which really just means, *Black girl didn't follow the rules. She peered into Bluebeard's closet and discovered the bodies swinging.*

When held up to the light, my bones, toothpick thin (sanded down). Ancestors stood over the pot sucking their teeth saying, *this will not do. She won't survive.* Being body-less, ancestors could not offer their bones to fuse my skeleton <u>thicker</u>. But being drenched in folk-years—they could offer a slither of something, a morsel of <u>trouble</u>—the good kind.

Re-crafted on a Sunday, the moon was bloody—earth, fire, water & air, were there to witness.

It was creation-time, so all the extras were happening—the stars were winking, the leaves rubbed each other loudly, while the worms, the serpents of the soil, wiggled softening the ground. Everything was wet & moaning— history moving in & out (forward & backward) grinding on black holes until suddenly—stillness attended with a soft sigh.

There was thunder & red serpents, like blistering veins—but myth always attends re-makings. There were screams sonic & soulful chiming the needles of pine trees & the lantern that only asks for blood teemed. Grandma says, *no amount of oil can silence the hinges of haunted closets—& yet, & yet* . . .

What do you call the half point between tomorrow & yesterday when dawn snakes out of its red silk dress? I have words, *honey, I'll split you in two.*

THICKness & TROUBLEless

TROUBLE US THICK WITH TROUBLE THICK WITH TROUBLE THICK WITH TROUBLE THICK WITH TROUBLE THICK WITH TROUBLE THICK WITH TROUBLE THICK WITH TROUBLE THICK WITH TROUBLE THICK WITH TROUBLE **LOVE US** WITH TROUBLE THICK WITH TROUBLE THICK WITH TROUBLE THICK WITH TROUBLE THICK WITH TROUBLE THICK WITH TROUBLE THICK WITH TROUBLE THICK WITH TROUBLE THICK WITH TROUBLE THICK WITH TROUBLE THICK WITH TROUBLE THICK WITH TROUBLE **LORE US** THICK WITH TROUBLE THICK WITH TROUBLE THICK WITH TROUBLE THICK WITH TROUBLE THICK WITH TROUBLE THICK WITH TROUBLE THICK WITH TROUBLE THICK WITH TROUBLE THICK WITH **BLEED US** THICK WITH TROUBLE THICK WITH TROUBLE THICK WITH TROUBLE THICK WITH TROUBLE THICK WITH TROUBLE THICK WITH TROUBLE THICK WITH TROUBLE THICK WITH TROUBLE THICK WITH TROUBLE THICK WITH TROUBLE THICK WITH TROUBLE THICK WITH TROUBLE THICK WITH TROUBLE THICK WITH TROUBLE THICK WITH TROUBLE **LANTERN US** WITH TROUBLE THICK WITH TROUBLE THICK WITH TROUBLE THICK WITH TROUBLE THICK WITH TROUBLE **HAUNT US** WITH TROUBLE THICK WITH TROUBLE THICK WITH TROUBLE THICK WITH TROUBLE THICK WITH TROUBLE THICK WITH TROUBLE THICK WITH TROUBLE THICK WITH **WITCH US** THICK WITH TROUBLE THICK WITH TROUBLE THICK WITH TROUBLE THICK WITH TROUBLE THICK WITH TROUBLE THICK WITH TROUBLE THICK WITH TROUBLE THICK WITH TROUBLE THICK WITH TROUBLE **THICK US** WITH TROUBLE THICK WITH TROUBLE THICK WITH TROUBLE THICK WITH TROUBLE THICK WITH TROUBLE THICK WITH TROUBLE THICK WITH TROUBLE THICK WITH TROUBLE THICK **GHOST US** THICK WITH TROUBLE THICK WITH TROUBLE THICK WITH TROUBLE THICK WITH TROUBLE THICK WITH TROUBLE THICK WITH TROUBLE THICK WITH TROUBLE THICK WITH TROUBLE THICK WITH TROUBLE THICK THICK WITH TROUBLE THICK WITH

REMEMBER US?
GOSPEL US
INTO FOLKLORE

Acknowledgments

Many thanks to the following for publishing earlier versions of the poems in this collection:

Boulevard: "New Tarot Names for Black Girls"
The Cincinnati Review: "Eulogy for Blood Left Behind"
decomp: "Black Witch Moth"
Pretty Owl Poetry: "Abracadabra"
Provincetown Arts: "Neophyte Psalm"
Rust & Moth: "I Won't Let Anyone (Black) Die Alone"
Virginia Quarterly Review: "For Black Kids Building Up Their Bones"
Willow Springs Magazine: "Southern Gothic (Come Sit)"

First, boundless gratitude to the ancestors who always follow my lifeline closely. Infinite adoration to the women who raised me. Mario and Debra, thank you for your steadfast love and guidance.

To my brilliant teachers and friends, Dr. Joanne Gabbin, John Skoyles, Inman Majors, Monica DiMuzio, Chris Baron, and Laurie Kutchins, thank you for your encouragement and for helping me discover my voice as a poet. Special shout-out to my Writing Coven, Furious Flower Poetry Center and YA novel in verse writer friends—I adore you.

Thank you to my editor, Allie Merola—your guidance and notes have been priceless.

Thank you, reader, for sitting with these pages—I am always wishing you wellness and joy.

AMBER McBRIDE is the author of *Gone Wolf, We Are All So Good at Smiling,* and *Me (Moth)*, a young adult novel that was a finalist for the National Book Award for Young People's Literature and won the 2022 Coretta Scott King–John Steptoe Award for New Talent. Her work has been published in *Ploughshares* and *Provincetown Arts*, among other publications. She is a professor of English and creative writing at the University of Virginia.

PENGUIN POETS

PENGUIN POETS

PHILLIS LEVIN
May Day
Mr. Memory & Other Poems

PATRICIA LOCKWOOD
Motherland Fatherland
  Homelandsexuals

WILLIAM LOGAN
Rift of Light

J. MICHAEL MARTINEZ
Museum of the Americas
Tarta Americana

ADRIAN MATEJKA
The Big Smoke
Map to the Stars
Mixology
Somebody Else Sold the World

AMBER McBRIDE
Thick with Trouble

MICHAEL McCLURE
Huge Dreams: San Francisco
  and Beat Poems

ROSE McLARNEY
Colorfast
Forage
Its Day Being Gone

DAVID MELTZER
David's Copy: The Selected
  Poems of David Meltzer

TERESA K. MILLER
Borderline Fortune

ROBERT MORGAN
Dark Energy
Terroir

CAROL MUSKE-DUKES
Blue Rose
An Octave Above Thunder:
  New and Selected Poems
Red Trousseau
Twin Cities

ALICE NOTLEY
Being Reflected Upon
Certain Magical Acts
Culture of One
The Descent of Alette
Disobedience
For the Ride
In the Pines
Mysteries of Small Houses

WILLIE PERDOMO
The Crazy Bunch
The Essential Hits of
  Shorty Bon Bon

DANIEL POPPICK
Fear of Description

LIA PURPURA
It Shouldn't Have Been
  Beautiful

LAWRENCE RAAB
The History of Forgetting
Visible Signs:
  New and Selected Poems

BARBARA RAS
The Last Skin
One Hidden Stuff

MICHAEL ROBBINS
Alien vs. Predator
The Second Sex
Walkman

PATTIANN ROGERS
Flickering
Generations
Holy Heathen Rhapsody
Quickening Fields
Wayfare

SAM SAX
Madness

ROBYN SCHIFF
Information Desk:
  An Epic
A Woman of Property

WILLIAM STOBB
Absentia
Nervous Systems

TRYFON TOLIDES
An Almost Pure Empty
  Walking

VINCENT TORO
Tertulia

PAUL TRAN
All the Flowers Kneeling

SARAH VAP
Viability

ANNE WALDMAN
Gossamurmur
Kill or Cure
Manatee/Humanity
Trickster Feminism

JAMES WELCH
Riding the Earthboy 40

PHILIP WHALEN
Overtime: Selected Poems

PHILLIP B. WILLIAMS
Mutiny

ROBERT WRIGLEY
Anatomy of Melancholy and
  Other Poems
Beautiful Country
Box
Earthly Meditations:
  New and Selected Poems
Lives of the Animals
Reign of Snakes
The True Account of Myself
  as a Bird

MARK YAKICH
The Importance of Peeling
  Potatoes in Ukraine
Spiritual Exercises
Unrelated Individuals Forming
  a Group Waiting to Cross